EXPLORING DINOSAURS

ANKYLOSAURUS

By Susan H. Gray

THE CHILD'S WORLD
CHANHASSEN, MINNESOTA

Published in the United States of America by The Child's World®
P.O. Box 326, Chanhassen, MN 55317-0326
800-599-READ
www.childsworld.com

Content Adviser:
Peter Makovicky,
Ph.D., Curator,
Field Museum,
Chicago, Illinois

Photo Credits: Rick Edwards, Dept. of Paleontology, American Museum of Natural History: 12; Peter McFarren/AP/Wide World Photos: 18; Kevin Schafer/Corbis: 6; Bettmann/Corbis: 11, 13, 20; Jonathan Blair/Corbis: 23; Stephen J. Krasemann/Photo Researchers, Inc.: 5; Francois Gohier/Photo Researchers, Inc.: 7, 10, 14, 15, 19, 22, 27; Sinclair Stammers/Science Photo Library/Photo Researchers, Inc.: 17; Charles V. Angelo/Photo Researchers, Inc.: 21; Joe Tucciarone/Science Photo Library/Photo Researchers, Inc.: 25; Albert J. Copley/Visuals Unlimited: 8, 9.

The Child's World®: Mary Berendes, Publishing Director

Editorial Directions, Inc.: E. Russell Primm, Editorial Director; Dana Meachen Rau, Line Editor; Katie Marsico, Assistant Editor; Matthew Messbarger, Editorial Assistant; Susan Hindman, Copy Editor; Susan Ashley, Proofreader; Tim Griffin, Indexer; Kerry Reid, Fact Checker; Dawn Friedman, Photo Reseacher; Linda S. Koutris, Photo Selector

Original cover art by Todd Marshall

The Design Lab: Kathleen Petelinsek, Design and Page Production

Library of Congress Cataloging-in-Publication Data
Gray, Susan Heinrichs.
  Ankylosaurus / by Susan H. Gray.
    p. cm. — (Exploring dinosaurs)
Includes index.
Summary: Describes what is known about the physical characteristics, behavior, habitat, and life cycle of this armor-plated dinosaur.
  ISBN 1-59296-042-1 (lib. bdg. : alk. paper)
  1. Ankylosaurus—Juvenile literature. [1. Ankylosaurus. 2. Dinosaurs.] I. Title.
QE862.O65G745 2004
567.915—dc22   2003018629

TABLE OF CONTENTS

CHAPTER ONE

HAVING TO EAT
AND RUN

The afternoon rain slowed to a sprinkle. Sunlight peeked

through the clouds. *Ankylosaurus* (AN-kuh-low-SORE-uhss)

stood in a patch of moss, slowly chewing away. He blinked as rain-

drops hit the heavy ridges above his eyes.

Ankylosaurus heard a loud splash behind him. He swung his

heavy, clubbed tail, but hit nothing. Another splash. He turned his

head to look back. But with his thick armor, he could not turn far

enough to see. Splash! *Ankylosaurus* started walking away on his

stubby legs, then sped up into a trot. His broad feet pounded the

earth and splashed mud everywhere. For a big, heavy dinosaur, he

was moving!

He reached a grove of trees and slowed to a stop. He was

Despite being a peaceful, plant-eating dinosaur, Ankylosaurus *was a huge, armored tank of a fighter. It weighed about 4 to 6 tons and could hold its own against enemies with its spike-covered body and battering-ram-like tail.*

Because Ankylosaurus *was built low to the ground, it had to eat lots of low-lying plants, such as ferns. This fossilized fern is one kind of plant that an* Ankylosaurus *would have munched on.*

panting, his huge, leathery sides heaving in and out. Here in the shade grew some delicious ferns. *Ankylosaurus* completely forgot why he had been running, and buried his head in the plants. Meanwhile, back at the moss patch, birds kept splashing away in the puddles.

CHAPTER TWO

WHAT IS AN ANKYLOSAURUS?

The *Ankylosaurus* is a dinosaur that lived from about 72 million to 65 million years ago. Its name is taken from Greek words that mean "stiff lizard" or "fused lizard." The name refers to the many bony plates that covered its back and tail. These were fused, or joined together, with its thick skin, making the animal stiff.

The **reptile** had an excellent coat of armor. In addition to its heavy plates, it was also covered

*These rough, hard, bony plates covered almost every square inch of the Ankylosaurus. They helped fend off attacks from vicious **predators** such as the Tyrannosaurus rex.*

The only area of the Ankylosaurus *that was not covered in tough, bony plates and pointy spines was its underbelly. Flipping it over was the only way to disarm the dinosaur.*

with many short, thick spines. Rows of spines ran down the animal's

back from the neck to the tail. *Ankylosaurus* might also have had

another row of spines down each of its sides. Large spikes stuck out

from its head. A hard, bony shelf above each eye protected the

dinosaur's vision. *Ankylosaurus* even had bony eyelids.

Imagine getting zonked on the head with an Ankylosaurus *tail! This tail was as much a weapon as a body part. It provided the* Ankylosaurus *with one of nature's best designed defenses against predators.*

For more protection, *Ankylosaurus* had a mighty "club." Its muscular tail ended in a thick clump of bone, which was covered with tough, leathery skin. The tail was flexible enough to swing this bony club from side to side. One good, forceful swing was enough to break the shin or foot of an attacker.

Ankylosaurus is not known for having been the smartest of the dinosaurs. In fact, its intelligence was low compared to other dinosaurs.

Ankylosaurus reached about 30 feet (9.1 meters) in length.

It probably weighed between 4 and 6 tons. Its head was nearly

3 feet (0.9 m) long. Its skull bones were very thick, leaving little

space for a brain.

The dinosaur walked on four mighty legs. The back legs were

longer than the front legs, so the dinosaur's back sloped downward

toward its head. Because of its body shape and thick armor,

Ankylosaurus could not lift its head up very high. It probably could not stand on its hind legs.

Ankylosaurus was not built

for attacking other dinosaurs.

But it certainly was built to

defend itself against them.

    Ankylosaurus bones were

first discovered by a group

of fossil hunters in Montana.

A man named Barnum Brown

led the group. Brown gave the

dinosaur its name in 1908. So

far, parts of three *Ankylosaurus*

skeletons have been found in

North America.

Barnum Brown spent his whole life hunting for and studying dinosaur bones. He is considered to have been the closest thing to a real life Indiana Jones! He traveled all over the world in search of answers to the great mysteries of the dinosaur age.

NOTES OF A DINOSAUR HUNTER

"Passed Wilbur Titus herding a band of sheep . . . he was just as dirty as ever . . . Pete and Lambert took wagon and Billy and went . . . to prospect *Ankylosaurus* quarry for more fragments . . . *Ankylosaurus?* skull + frags [fragments] 2 miles below Tolman ferry right bank 100 ft. above river . . . Loaded skull and got part way to ranch got stuck . . . . Took out *Ankylosaurus* frags . . . Rain + snow . . . Packed remaining boxes . . . Waited for roads to dry."

These are just a few of the writings in Barnum Brown's field notes. Good scientists always write plenty of notes when they are working. Scientists work in laboratories, in libraries, and out in nature. When they are working out in nature, they say

June 8th 1908

Left Miles City about 3:30 P.M. after spending Friday, Saturday and Sunday there.

Had considerable difficulty in hiring a cook; finally engaged a man by name of C. H. Lambert an old ex cowpuncher at $50. per month.

Also had trouble in getting a saddle pony. Never saw horses as high or as scarce especially in one of the first horse markets of the world.

Found roads on Sunday Creek very soft and spongy and muddy in places. Camped about 2 miles beyond the 4 mile bridge.

June 9th

they are "in the field." So their notes are called field notes.

Brown (at left in the photograph) was one of the greatest dinosaur hunters ever. He began working for the American Museum of Natural History in New York when he was in his twenties. He got to travel all over the world searching for fossils. Brown always liked to dress nicely, even when he was working in the field. Everyone else would wear old clothes and get dirty, but not Brown. He wore a nice hat, coat, and tie in the field.

Brown led several crews on dinosaur hunts. They worked for years in Wyoming, Montana, and Alberta, Canada. With all this hard work, it is not surprising that he found so many fossils. He discovered not only *Ankylosaurus*, but also the first *Tyrannosaurus rex* (tie-RAN-uh-SORE-uhss REX). Thanks to his field notes, we know what hard work it was to make these discoveries.

CHAPTER THREE

DINOSAUR DIETS

Several things about *Ankylosaurus* tell us that it was a plant eater, or herbivore (UR-buh-vore). Its teeth were small and wide, not long and pointy. These teeth were good for grinding plant materials, not for biting meat. Its snout ended in a beak with a hard covering. Such a beak would have been good for tearing plants from the ground or leaves from bushes. The animal's heavy body, built

This fossil of an Araucaria cone is a key to the past. It helps scientists learn about what dinosaurs like Ankylosaurus might have eaten. Fossils are nature's time capsules. They preserve the history of our planet for future generations to see.

close to the ground, would not have been fast enough to chase

down **prey.**

Ankylosaurus was big and wide at the waist and hips. This also

tells us that the animal ate plants. Plants contain a lot of material

called cellulose (SELL-yoo-loce). Cellulose is hard to digest.

Because the Ankylosaurus *ate so many plants, scientists think it probably had
a special compartment to help it digest all of the tough plant material.
This would have made it produce lots and lots of gas!*

Plant-eating animals have special **adaptations** (ad-ap-TAY-shuns) to help them digest cellulose. They may have an extra stomach or very long intestines. These take up lots of space in an animal's body. So the animal is big and wide. Because *Ankylosaurus* was so wide, scientists think it was adapted for a diet of plants.

Ankylosaurus also had special adaptations to keep from being eaten. The bony plates and spines on its back were protection against the teeth and claws of predators. Smaller plates shielded its face and eyes. Only the animal's underside was unprotected. Its belly and throat had no spines at all. If *Ankylosaurus* were flipped over on its side or back, it would have been in trouble. But the animal was too heavy and low to the ground for most attackers to do this.

CHAPTER FOUR

MAKING TRACKS

Paleontologists (PAY-lee-un-TAWL-uh-jists) are people who study **ancient** plant and animal life. They often study fossils. These are remains of plants and animals that lived long, long ago. Dinosaur fossils include skeletons, eggs, and footprints.

Until recently, most paleontologists thought *Ankylosaurus* was a

Paleontologists have found many fossilized dinosaur eggs at more than 200 sites in the United States, France, Spain, Argentina, India, Mongolia, and China.

slow-moving dinosaur. They believed that something so big and heavy

could only lumber along slowly. But in 1998, a paleontologist named

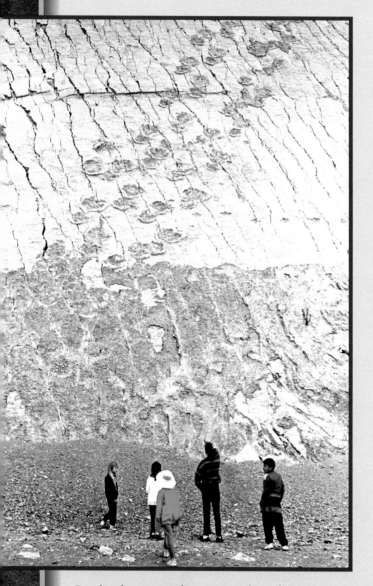

Christian Meyer found foot-

prints that told a different

story. Meyer was leading a

group of scientists on a field

trip. They were in the South

American country of Bolivia.

There, they found a huge area

covered with dinosaur track-

ways. Trackways are sets of

dinosaur footprints. The area

was more than 6 acres (2.4

*People who want to know more about dinosaurs
flock to Bolivia to get an up-close look at the
dinosaur tracks. Imagine seeing the actual footprints
of dinosaurs that once roamed that very land!*

hectares) in size. It quickly

became famous for having the

most dinosaur trackways in

the world.

Meyer and his team

counted more than 250 different

sets of footprints. They could

tell that six different kinds of

dinosaurs had made the prints.

Researchers who study dinosaur tracks say that tracks are the closest we can get to understanding dinosaurs as living, breathing animals. Tracks tell much about where and how dinosaurs walked, as well as which dinosaurs roamed alone and which moved in groups.

They saw that some dinosaurs had been walking normally. Some had

been limping. And some appeared to be trotting rather quickly.

The team decided that some of the footprints belonged to the

group of dinosaurs called ankylosaurs (*Ankylosaurus* and its relatives).

They figured that some were able to run at about 8 miles (12.8 kilo-

meters) per hour.

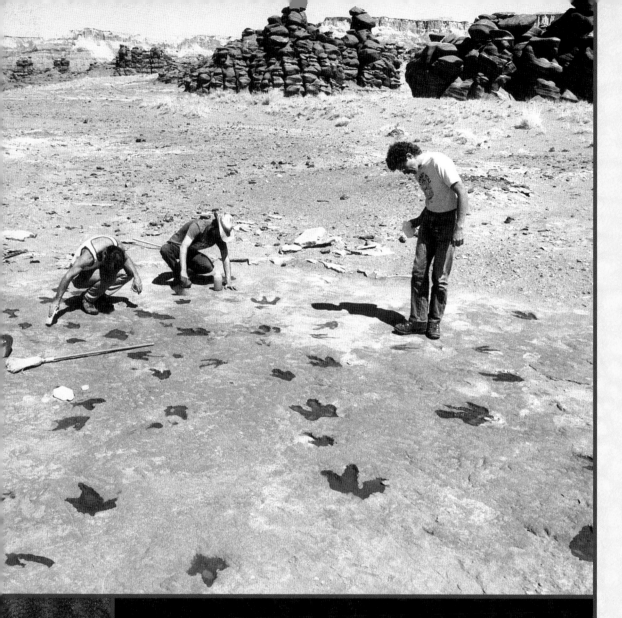

STUDYING TRACKWAYS

Paleontologists can tell a lot about a dinosaur just by looking at its tracks. If a big groove follows the footprints, they know the dinosaur dragged its tail as it walked. If one foot made a light print over and over, they know the dinosaur was limping.

If the dinosaur took extra long steps, scientists think it was probably running. Sometimes scientists study elephants and hippopotamuses to see how they run. They might measure the legs of these animals and compare them to dinosaur legs. They might check to see how far apart their footprints are. Scientists then use this knowledge to tell them about dinosaur footprints. It helps them figure out how fast dinosaurs could run.

The ankylosaur trackways in Bolivia surprised the paleontologists. They showed that this group of dinosaurs moved much faster than anyone had ever thought.

CHAPTER FIVE

LIFE IN THE CRETACEOUS PERIOD

Ankylosaurus walked the Earth during a time called the Cretaceous (kreh-TAY-shuss) period. The whole period lasted from 144 million years to 65 million years ago. But *Ankylosaurus* was around for only a few million years of that time.

Dinosaurs first appeared on Earth about 230 million years ago. These were small creatures that ran on two legs. In time, more and more dinosaurs appeared. Some grew quite large. Some walked on four legs. *Ankylosaurus* was one of the big, four-legged dinosaurs.

Coelophysis *(pronounced SEE-low-FIE-sis) was a small dinosaur with a tiny skull. It had a long, pointed head with lots of small teeth.* Coelophysis *lived in a different period than* Ankylosaurus.

During the Cretaceous period, many reptiles roamed the Earth. Dinosaurs, snakes, and lizards were common on the ground. Flying reptiles called pterosaurs (TEHR-uh-sorz) soared

Snakes existed on Earth at the same time as the dinosaurs. Snakes first appeared during the late Cretaceous period (about 95 million years ago), towards the end of the time of the dinosaurs.

overhead. Swimming reptiles lived in the oceans.

Not all animals were reptiles, though. Small mammals not much bigger than rats darted about on the forest floor. Feathered birds flew from tree to tree. Sharks, rays, and other fish glided through the ocean waters.

CHAPTER SIX

So What Happened?

Something big happened at the end of the Cretaceous period, but no one knows what it was. Paleontologists tell us that 65 million years ago, dinosaurs became **extinct.** All over the world, they just died out. At about the same time, the pterosaurs, the reptiles of the sea, and many other animals disappeared. What could have caused this to happen?

Scientists have a few ideas. A lot of volcanoes were erupting at the end of the Cretaceous period. Perhaps this changed the air so much that dinosaurs could no longer breathe. Maybe the dinosaurs could not find enough food. Perhaps heat waves, diseases, or egg-eating mammals wiped the dinosaurs out. Over the years, scientists have thought a lot about what killed all the dinosaurs.

There is one more idea that has gotten a lot of attention.

Some scientists believe a giant **asteroid** crashed into Earth about

65 million years ago. They feel that such a crash could have caused

many different kinds of animals to die out. But how?

*Asteroids can be as small as pebbles or as large as 578 miles (930 km) in diameter.
Sixteen of the 3,000 known asteroids are more than 150 miles (240 km) in
diameter. Some asteroids even have their own orbiting moons.*

In the 1970s and 1980s, scientists began to notice something unusual in rocks from around the world. The rocks from about 65 million years ago had a lot of a material called iridium (ih-RID-ee-um) in them. Iridium is very rare on Earth. But asteroids hurtling through space have plenty of it. If an asteroid slammed into Earth, it would release iridium over a huge area.

This is what many scientists believe happened 65 million years ago. A giant asteroid traveling at thousands of miles an hour crashed into the Earth. The iridium and dust from the crash spread every-where. Skies darkened, and many animals died.

This does not explain everything, though. It does not explain how plants survived. It does not explain why some animals lived on. The birds we know today, for example, are relatives of the dinosaurs. The birds survived, yet dinosaurs such as *Ankylosaurus* did not.

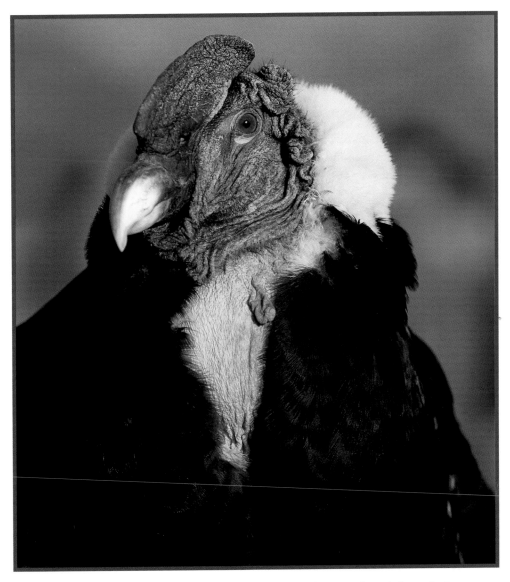

Why did the dinosaurs die out and birds like this condor stay alive? Paleontologists may never know, but mysteries like this make studying dinosaurs fun.

The mystery of the great extinction might never be answered.

All we know is that something big happened 65 million years ago.

And because of it, not a single dinosaur was left on Earth.

Glossary

adaptations (ad-ap-TAY-shuhnz) Adaptations are adjustments to something in the environment. Plant-eating animals have special adaptations to help them digest cellulose.

ancient (AYN-shunt) Something that is ancient is very old; from millions of years ago. Paleontology is the study of ancient plant and animal life.

asteroid (ASS-tuh-roid) An asteroid is a rocky body that is smaller than a planet and orbits the sun. A giant asteroid may have crashed into Earth millions of years ago and caused the dinosaurs to die out.

extinct (ek-STINGKT) Something that is extinct no longer exists. The dinosaurs became extinct about 65 million years ago.

predators (PRED-uh-turz) Predators are animals that hunt and eat other animals. The bony plates and spines of *Ankylosaurus* helped protect them from predators.

prey (PRAY) Prey are animals that are hunted and eaten by other animals. The bulky body of *Ankylosaurus* would have made it difficult for the dinosaur to chase after prey.

reptile (REP-tile) A reptile is an air-breathing animal with a backbone and is usually covered with scales or plates. *Ankylosaurus* was an example of a reptile.

Did You Know?

▸ Ankylosaur trackways have been found in several places in the world. Except for the trackways in Bolivia, they all show that *Ankylosaurus* was a slow mover.

▸ *Ankylosaurus* had a very small brain for its body. Many scientists take this to mean that the dinosaur was not very smart.

▸ The full name of the dinosaur found by Barnum Brown is *Ankylosaurus magniventris* (MAG-nih-VEN-triss). This name means "stiff lizard with a big belly"!

The Geologic Time Scale

TRIASSIC PERIOD

Date: 248 million to 208 million years ago

Fossils: *Coelophysis, Cynodont, Desmatosuchus, Eoraptor, Gerrothorax, Peteinosaurus, Placerias, Plateosaurus, Postosuchus, Procompsognathus, Riojasaurus, Saltopus, Teratosaurus, Thecodontosaurus*

Distinguishing Features: For the most part, the climate in the Triassic period was hot and dry. The first true mammals appeared during this period, as well as turtles, frogs, salamanders, and lizards. Corals could also be found in oceans at this time, although large reefs such as the ones we have today did not yet exist. Evergreen trees made up much of the plant life.

JURASSIC PERIOD

Date: 208 million to 144 million years ago

Fossils: *Allosaurus, Anchisaurus, Apatosaurus, Barosaurus, Brachiosaurus, Ceratosaurus, Compsognathus, Cryptoclidus, Dilophosaurus, Diplodocus, Eustreptospondylus, Hybodus, Janenschia, Kentrosaurus, Liopleurodon, Megalosaurus, Opthalmosaurus, Rhamphorhynchus, Saurolophus, Segisaurus, Seismosaurus, Stegosaurus, Supersaurus, Syntarsus, Ultrasaurus, Vulcanodon, Xiaosaurus*

Distinguishing Features: The climate of the Jurassic period was warm and moist. The first birds appeared during this period. Plant life was also greener and more widespread. Sharks began swimming in Earth's oceans. Although dinosaurs didn't even exist at the beginning of the Triassic period, they ruled Earth by Jurassic times. There was a minor mass extinction toward the end of the Jurassic period.

CRETACEOUS PERIOD

Date: 144 million to 65 million years ago

Fossils: *Acrocanthosaurus, Alamosaurus, Albertosaurus, Anatotitan, Ankylosaurus, Argentinosaurus, Bagaceratops, Baryonyx, Carcharodontosaurus, Carnotaurus, Centrosaurus, Chasmosaurus, Corythosaurus, Didelphodon, Edmontonia, Edmontosaurus, Gallimimus, Gigantosaurus, Hadrosaurus, Hypsilophodon, Iguanodon, Kronosaurus, Lambeosaurus, Leaellynasaura, Maiasaura, Megaraptor, Muttaburrasaurus, Nodosaurus, Ornithocheirus, Oviraptor, Pachycephalosaurus, Panoplosaurus, Parasaurolophus, Pentaceratops, Polacanthus, Protoceratops, Psittacosaurus, Quaesitosaurus, Saltasaurus, Sarcosuchus, Saurolophus, Sauropelta, Saurornithoides, Segnosaurus, Spinosaurus, Stegoceras, Stygimoloch, Styracosaurus, Tapejara, Tarbosaurus, Therizinosaurus, Thescelosaurus, Torosaurus, Trachodon, Triceratops, Troodon, Tyrannosaurus rex, Utahraptor, Velociraptor*

Distinguishing Features: The climate of the Cretaceous period was fairly mild. Flowering plants first appeared in this period, and many modern plants developed. With flowering plants came a greater diversity of insect life. Birds further developed into two types: flying and flightless. A wider variety of mammals also existed. At the end of this period came a great mass extinction that wiped out the dinosaurs, along with several other groups of animals.

How to Learn More

At the Library

Holmes, Thom, Laurie Holmes, and Michael William Skrepnick (illustrator).
Armored, Plated, and Bone-Headed Dinosaurs: The Ankylosaurs, Stegosaurs, and Pachycephalosaurs.
Berkeley Heights, N.J.: Enslow Publishers, Inc., 2002.

Oliver, Rupert, and Bernard Long (illustrator). *Ankylosaurus.*
Vero Beach, Fla.: The Rourke Book Company, Inc., 2001.

On the Web

Visit our home page for lots of links about *Ankylosaurus:*
http://www.childsworld.com/links.html
Note to Parents, Teachers, and Librarians: We routinely verify our
Web links to make sure they're safe, active sites—so encourage
your readers to check them out!

Places to Visit or Contact

AMERICAN MUSEUM OF NATURAL HISTORY
*To view numerous dinosaur fossils, as well as
the fossils of several ancient mammals*
Central Park West at 79th Street
New York, NY 10024-5192
212/769-5100

CARNEGIE MUSEUM OF NATURAL HISTORY
*To view a variety of dinosaur skeletons, as well as fossils related
to other reptiles, amphibians, and fish that are now extinct*
4400 Forbes Avenue
Pittsburgh, PA 15213
412/622-3131

DINOSAUR NATIONAL MONUMENT
To view a huge deposit of dinosaur bones in a natural setting
4545 East Highway 40
Dinosaur, CO 81610-9724
or
DINOSAUR NATIONAL MONUMENT (QUARRY)
11625 East 1500 South
Jensen, UT 84035
435/781-7700

MUSEUM OF THE ROCKIES
To see real dinosaur fossils, as well as robotic replicas
Montana State University
600 West Kagy Boulevard
Bozeman, MT 59717-2730
406/994-2251 or 406/994-DINO (3466)

NATIONAL MUSEUM OF NATURAL HISTORY
(SMITHSONIAN INSTITUTION)
To see several dinosaur exhibits and take special behind-the-scenes tours
10th Street and Constitution Avenue, N.W.
Washington, DC 20560-0166
202/357-2700

Index

About the Author

Susan H. Gray has bachelor's and master's degrees in zoology, and has taught college-level courses in biology. She first fell in love with fossil hunting while studying paleontology in college. In her 25 years as an author, she has written many articles for scientists and researchers, and many science books for children. Susan enjoys gardening, traveling, and playing the piano. She and her husband, Michael, live in Cabot, Arkansas.